Thank you for choosing our journal!
We hope you enjoy it as much as we do.

We Invite you to check out our website
for more of our books:

www.TheJournalFolks.com

Made in the USA
Las Vegas, NV
10 May 2022

48688036R00076